Pennie Stoyles and Peter Pentland

The A to Z of
Inventions
and Inventors

Volume 6: T to Z

Smart Apple Media

This edition first published in 2006 in the United States of America by Smart Apple Media.

Smart Apple Media
2140 Howard Drive West
North Mankato
Minnesota 56003

First published in 2006 by
MACMILLAN EDUCATION AUSTRALIA PTY LTD
627 Chapel Street, South Yarra, Australia 3141

Visit our website at www.macmillan.com.au

Associated companies and representatives throughout the world.

Copyright © Pennie Stoyles and Peter Pentland 2006

Library of Congress Cataloging-in-Publication Data

Stoyles, Pennie.
    The A to Z of inventions and inventors / Pennie Stoyles and Peter Pentland.
    p. cm.
    Contents: v. 1 A to B – v. 2. C to F – v. 3. G to L – v. 4. M to P – v. 5. Q-S – v.6 T-Z.
    ISBN-13: 978-1-58340-804-9 (v. 1)
    ISBN-13: 978-1-58340-805-6 (v. 2)
    ISBN-13: 978-1-58340-788-2 (v. 3)
    ISBN-13: 978-1-58340-789-9 (v. 4)
    ISBN-13: 978-1-58340-790-5 (v. 5)
    ISBN-13: 978-1-58340-791-2 (v. 6)
    1. Inventions—History—20th century—Encyclopedias. 2. Inventors—Biography—Encyclopedias.
    I. Pentland, Peter. II. Title.
    T20.S76 2006
    608.03—dc22   2005057602

Edited by Sam Munday
Text and cover design by Ivan Finnegan, iF design
Page layout by Ivan Finnegan, iF design
Photo research by Legend Images
Illustrations by Alan Laver, Shelly Communications

Printed in USA

Acknowledgments

The author and the publisher are grateful to the following for permission to reproduce copyright material:

Front cover: photo of yo-yo courtesy of Brand X Pictures

Photos courtesy of:
The Advertising Archives, p. 5; Australian Picture Library/Corbis, pp. 6, 8 (bottom), 16; Hulton Archive/Getty Images, p. 10 (top); iStockphoto.com, p. 8 (top); Legendimages, p. 17 (left); Photolibrary/ Bildhuset Ab, p. 12; Photolibrary/Photo Researchers, Inc., p. 23; Photolibrary/Photonica Inc, p. 26; Photolibrary/Science Photo Library, p. 24; Photolibrary/Dr Jeremy Burgess/Science Photo Library, p. 22; Photolibrary/SuperStock, p. 28 (bottom); Photolibrary/Workbook, Inc., p. 30; Photoobjects, © 2005 JupiterImages Corporation, p. 7; Photos.com, pp. 10 (bottom), 18, 19; Rob Cruse Photography, p. 4; Science Museum/Science & Society Picture Library, p. 20; Tim Berners-Lee, p. 25; The Toaster Museum Foundation, used with permission, p. 14.

Please note
At the time of printing, the Internet addresses appearing in this book were correct. Owing to the dynamic nature of the Internet, however, we cannot guarantee that all these addresses will remain correct.

Inventions

Welcome to the exciting world of inventions.

The A to Z of Inventions and Inventors is about inventions that people use every day. Sometimes these inventions happen by accident. Sometimes they come from a moment of inspiration. Often they are developed from previous inventions. In some cases, inventors race against each other to invent a machine.

Volume 6: T to Z inventions

They said it!

"There's nothing on it worthwhile, and we're not going to watch it in this household, and I don't want it in your intellectual diet."

Philo T. Farnsworth's advice to his children about his invention, television.

Tea bag

A tea bag is a little paper bag of loose tea that can be used in a cup or a pot.

Who invented the tea bag?

The tea bag was invented by Thomas Sullivan, an American in about 1903.

The tea bag story

Thomas Sullivan was a tea and coffee merchant in New York. He used silk and **muslin** to make little bags of tea to give to his customers as samples. He noticed that some of his customers were putting the sample bags directly into the water to make tea. At this time, tea was made using loose tea leaves. By 1904, he was selling the tea bags to hotels and restaurants all around the world. By the 1930s, the bags were being used in people's homes and were made from paper instead of cloth.

Did you know?

Some people put cold tea bags on their eyes as a beauty treatment to prevent puffy eyes and wrinkles.

Tea bags come in several different shapes.

How tea bags work

Tea is made from the leaves of a tea bush. The leaves are picked and then dried. When the tea leaves are put in boiling water, the flavors seep out. When you use loose tea in a teapot there are messy tea leaves to clean up. The tea leaves in tea bags are finer than loose tea, so that the flavor can seep out more quickly. Tea bags are more convenient because they can be used in a cup and then thrown out without much mess.

A Teasmade allows you to have a cup of tea without leaving your bed.

Changes to tea bags over time

Since tea bags were invented, there have been many changes to their design. You can now buy four-sided tea bags which allow the flavor of the tea to seep out more quickly. Draw-string teabags can be squeezed so that they do not drip.

Related invention

An automatic tea-making machine was invented in 1937. It heated the water, made the tea, and then woke you with an alarm. It was originally called Cheerywake, but was renamed Teasmade.

Glossary word

muslin   a very fine cotton cloth

Telephone

The telephone uses electrical signals to send sounds and data through wires.

Who invented the telephone?

Alexander Graham Bell, a Scot living in the United States, invented the telephone in 1876.

The telephone story

Alexander Graham Bell and his assistant Thomas Watson developed the basic ideas for the telephone in 1874. On March 10, 1876, Bell sent the first telephone message all the way to the next room. He said: "Watson, come here. I want you."

Bell and Watson were not the only people trying to invent the telephone. Watson got to the **patent** office just two hours before another inventor who had developed a similar device.

Alexander Graham Bell makes the first long-distance call from New York to Chicago in 1892.

Alexander Graham Bell (1847–1922)

Alexander Graham Bell was born in Scotland on March 3, 1847. He moved to the U.S. in 1871. After inventing the telephone, Bell went on to invent hydrofoil boats and an artificial respirator.

How the telephone works

A telephone mouthpiece changes sound into an electrical signal. This signal is mixed with an electrical wave and sent by wire through the telephone network to the receiving telephone. Here, the original signal is separated from the electrical wave and made stronger. It is then sent to the earpiece, where it is changed back into sound.

Some modern telephones do not need a cord to attach them to the power supply.

Changes to the telephone over time

Telephone signals were originally electrical and were sent through wires. Today the signals are also sent using optical fibers, radio waves, and satellites.

Mobile telephones are smaller and have more features such as games, text messaging, cameras, and color liquid crystal displays.

Related invention

Dr. Martin Cooper invented the modern mobile telephone in 1973. He worked for the Motorola Company.

Television sets use radio waves to make moving pictures and sound.

Who invented television?

Many people were involved in creating television, but an American, Philo T. Farnsworth, is credited with inventing the main parts that made television possible.

The television story

Scottish engineer, John Logie Baird, invented a mechanical television in 1925. The pictures were pink and fuzzy.

In 1927 American, Philo T. Farnsworth, produced a working model of the electronic scanning system used in today's televisions.

In 1931 in the U.S., Vladimir Zworykin invented an electronic camera tube. The same year in England, Isaac Shoenberg worked on transmitters and receivers.

A modern television.

Philo T. Farnsworth (1906–1971)

Philo T. Farnsworth was born in a log cabin and rode to school on a horse. He was fascinated with electricity and came up with the idea for making pictures on a screen when he was 14 years old. The RCA company used his ideas to make television sets and he had to take them to court to get the money he deserved.

How television works

A television station changes pictures and sounds into separate electrical signals. These are sent to a transmitter that uses these signals to send out radio waves.

The television aerial picks up the radio waves and changes them back into electrical signals before sending them to the television set.

One part of the signal goes to a radio receiver to make sound through the speaker. The other part of the signal is sent to the picture tube to make the pictures.

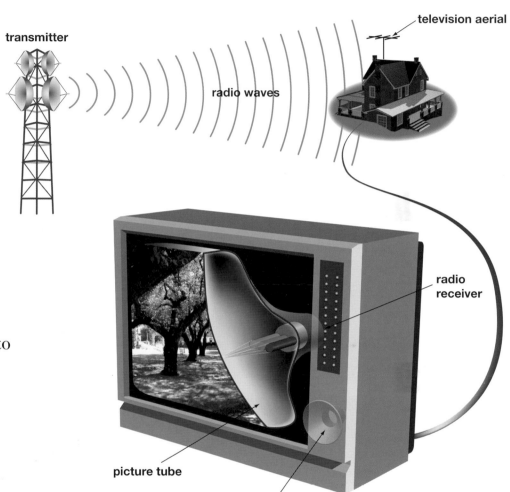

transmitter

television aerial

radio waves

radio receiver

picture tube

speaker

Changes to television over time

The first television sets made black and white pictures. Television pictures are now color and can be transmitted digitally through optical fiber cables into our homes. Flat screen LCD and plasma televisions are now available.

Related invention
Radio was invented by an Italian scientist, Guglielmo Marconi, in 1896.

Thermometer

Thermometers are instruments for measuring temperatures, or how hot or cold things are.

Who invented the thermometer?

Italian scientist, Galileo Galilei, invented the first type of thermometer in 1592.

Galileo Galilei (1564–1642) invented the thermometer.

The thermometer story

Galileo's thermometer had a glass bulb filled with air. The bulb was connected to a glass tube dipped into a colored liquid. When the air got hot it expanded and the liquid went farther along the tube.

The first example of a modern thermometer was developed in Italy in 1654. It had a water-filled glass bulb connected to a thin glass tube.

German scientist, Gabriel Fahrenheit, improved the thermometer by using mercury instead of water as the liquid.

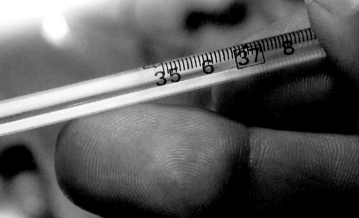

The temperature can be read on the side of a thermometer.

Thermometer timeline

1592	1612	1654	1714
Galileo made the first thermometer	Santorre Santorio used a thermometer to measure the temperature of patients	Water was used in the glass thermometer	Farenheit invented the glass thermometer containing mercury

How thermometers work

A thermometer has a thin glass tube connected to a bulb at the bottom. The bulb and tube contain a liquid, which is usually red-colored alcohol or silver-colored mercury.

When the liquid gets hot, it takes up more room. This pushes the top of the liquid farther up the tube. When the liquid cools down, it takes up less room and the top of the liquid moves down the tube. There are marks and numbers on the side of the tube so you can read the temperature accurately.

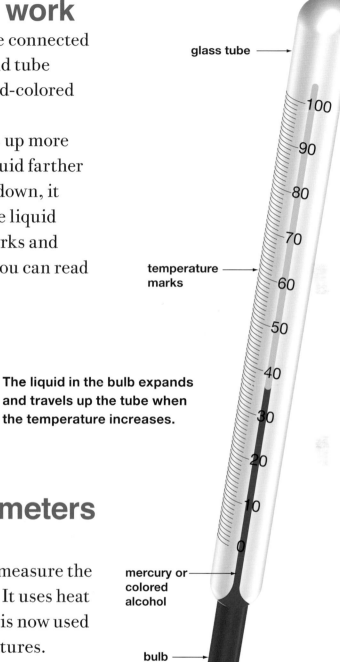

glass tube

temperature marks

The liquid in the bulb expands and travels up the tube when the temperature increases.

mercury or colored alcohol

bulb

Changes to thermometers over time

NASA developed a thermometer to measure the temperature of astronauts in space. It uses heat radiation given off inside the ear. It is now used to measure children's body temperatures.

Related inventions

Thermostats are mechanical devices used to control temperatures in buildings and machines. Dutch scientist, Cornelis Drebbel (1572–1634), invented the thermostat. He used it in an oven.

Thermos

A thermos is a container used to keep things hot or cold. It does this by preventing heat energy from moving into or out of the container.

Who invented the thermos?

British scientist, Sir James Dewar, invented the thermos in 1892.

The thermos story

Sir James Dewar was a science professor at Cambridge University. He was studying very cold liquids and needed a container to keep them cold.

Dewar produced a **vacuum** by removing all the air from a container. He was then able to invent the thermos. It consisted of two glass walls with a vacuum between them. This could keep the liquids cold as it would not allow heat to get inside.

One of Dewar's students, Rheinhold Burger, started to make thermoses for the public in 1904.

Thermoses can keep drinks hot or cold.

Did you know?

Burger couldn't think what to call his invention so he held a competition. The winner was "thermos," the Greek word for heat.

How thermoses work

A thermos has two glass sleeves joined together with a vacuum between them. The vacuum stops heat energy from being conducted into or out of the contents of the container.

The glass sleeves are coated with silver, just like a mirror. The mirror surfaces reflect heat back the way it came.

A thermos also has a lid over the container. It stops air from making contact with the contents of the container and carrying heat energy to or from them.

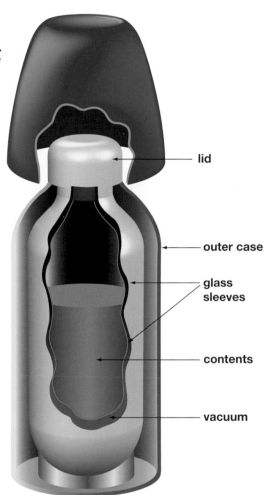

lid

outer case

glass sleeves

contents

vacuum

Changes to thermoses over time

Thermoses today have changed very little from the original design. Some now use stainless steel instead of glass for the sleeves.

Related invention

The Dewar flask was also invented by James Dewar. It is used to store liquid nitrogen.

Toaster

A toaster uses electricity to brown one or both sides of a slice of bread.

Who invented the toaster?

The first electric toaster was invented in 1893 in Great Britain by a company called Crompton and Co. In 1909, Frank Shailor from the General Electric Company of America patented the first electric toaster.

The toaster story

The General Electric Company of America released the first electric toaster, the D-12, onto the market in 1909. When one side was toasted, the bread was turned over by hand and the other side was toasted. The toast could be burned easily.

The pop-up toaster was invented by American Charles Strite in 1919. He made a machine that used a clockwork timer to turn off the electricity and release a spring that pushed the toast up when it was ready.

The D-12 electric toaster was first released in 1913.

Did you know?

It takes about as much electrical energy to toast a slice of bread as it takes to carry a 110-pound (50-kg) weight to the top of a 459-foot (140-m)-tall building.

How toasters work

The heating **element** inside the toaster has a length of wire wrapped around an electrically insulating plate. The wire becomes red hot when electricity flows through it.

The toaster has two or three heating elements. Sliced bread is lowered into a gap between the elements on a spring-loaded tray. The timer automatically cuts the flow of electricity through the elements and releases the spring when the toast is cooked. The spring raises the cooked toast.

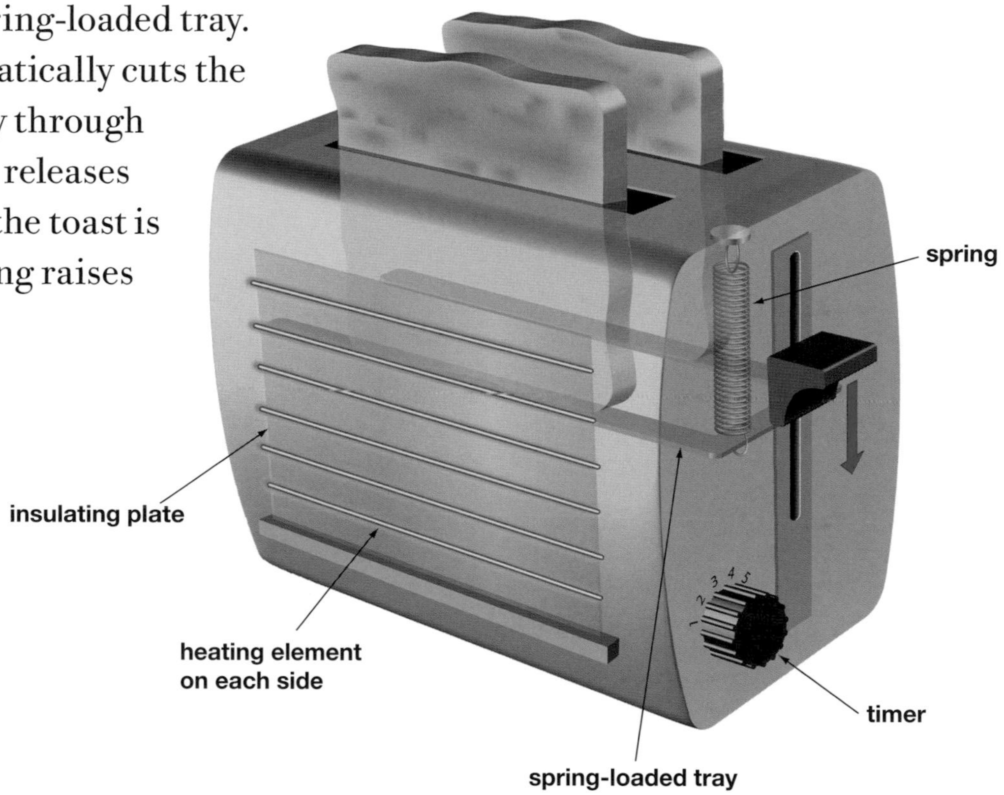

spring

insulating plate

heating element on each side

timer

spring-loaded tray

Changes to toasters over time

Some toasters are able to cook four slices of bread instead of just two.

Related invention

The invention of sliced bread in 1928, by American Otto Rohwedder, helped to make the toaster popular.

The flushing toilet uses water to flush away human waste. It is usually connected to a sewage system, where the waste is treated.

Who invented the toilet?

Nobody is sure exactly who invented the flushing toilet. It was probably invented by John Harrington in 1597, but has been improved over 400 years.

The toilet story

About 4,000 years ago many ancient peoples, including the Egyptians, Chinese, and Indians, had toilets that sat over flowing water. In 1597, John Harrington is believed to have made two flushing toilets. One was for his godmother Queen Elizabeth I and one was for himself. In 1885, an Englishman called Thomas Twyford built the first all-china flushing toilet.

The first china toilets were very decorative.

Toilet timeline

1852	1882	1942	1982	1998
The first public toilet was opened in a London street	Thomas Crapper invented the flushing mechanism that is still used today	Soft toilet paper rolls were invented	The dual flush toilet was invented	Automatic toilet seat cleaner was patented

How toilets work

Toilets have three main parts. The first part is the flusher which lets water flow from the cistern, or tank, into the bowl. The second part is the bowl and the pipe that leads from it. When the toilet is flushed, water enters the pipe. This acts like a **siphon** and sucks the water out of the bowl. The third part is the refill regulator which automatically turns the water on when you flush and turns the water off when the tank is full.

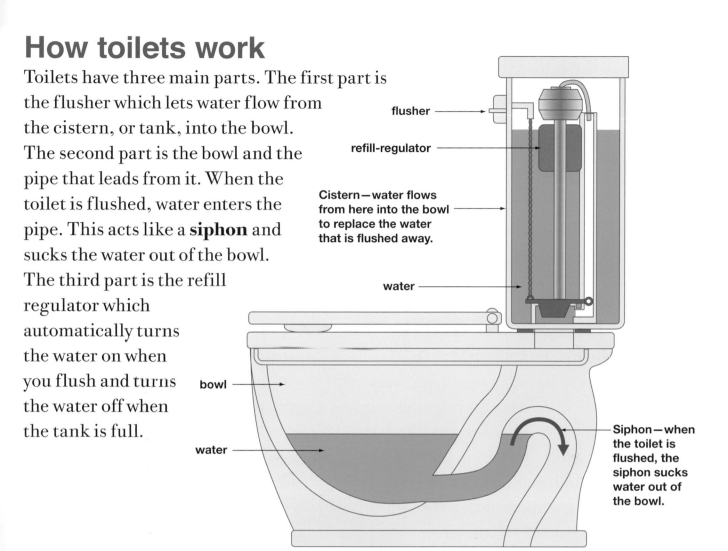

flusher

refill-regulator

Cistern—water flows from here into the bowl to replace the water that is flushed away.

water

bowl

water

Siphon—when the toilet is flushed, the siphon sucks water out of the bowl.

Changes to toilets over time

Engineers and scientists have been developing toilets that use less water. Older toilets use up to 21 pints (12 l) per flush. New dual-flush toilets use 11 pints (6 l) for a full flush and only 5 pints (3 l) for a half flush.

Related invention

In 1867, three brothers called Thomas, Edward, and Clarence Scott, invented **perforated** toilet paper.

Glossary words

siphon   a U-shaped pipe or tube for draining liquids
perforated   pierced with little holes, making sections which are easy to tear off

Uu Umbrella

An umbrella is a folding shade carried as protection from the sun or rain.

Who invented the umbrella?

Nobody is sure who invented umbrellas because they have been around for thousands of years. In 1874 an Englishman called Samuel Fox invented the first umbrella with steel ribs.

The umbrella story

Umbrellas are an ancient invention and they were originally used as sunshades. In many countries, umbrellas were carried by slaves to shade their masters and an umbrella was a sign of importance. Umbrellas were introduced to Europe in the 1500s. They were made of leather, the handles were wood or ivory, and the ribs were made from whalebone. In 1874, Samuel Fox ran a company that made steel products. He invented the hinged steel ribs that we see in umbrellas today.

Umbrellas keep you dry on rainy days.

 *Did you know?*

The word "umbrella" comes from the Latin word "umbra" which means shadow. The word "parasol" comes from two Latin words "pare" and "sol" which means "prepare for the sun."

How umbrellas work

The umbrella unfolds to create a barrier between the person carrying it and the rain or sun. The fabric sections of umbrellas are called "prevents." They are made of plastic or a fabric that has been treated with a waterproofing chemical. The ribs have hinges that fold up when the umbrella is closed. Folding or collapsible umbrellas have extra hinged joints in the ribs and the handle can slide into itself.

Metal ribs for umbrellas were invented in 1874.

Changes to umbrellas over time

In 1927 a German called Hans Haupt invented the first collapsible umbrella that could be folded down and carried in a bag. Ultra-collapsible umbrellas that fit into a zippered hard case are now available. There is also a model with a flashlight built into the case.

Related invention

In 1823 Charles Macintosh, a Scottish chemist, patented a method for making waterproof garments. It used rubber that was layered between two pieces of cloth. The mackintosh raincoat was named after him.

Vacuum cleaner

The vacuum cleaner is an electrical appliance that cleans using suction.

Who invented the vacuum cleaner?

The vacuum cleaner was invented in England, by Hubert Booth, in 1901.

The vacuum cleaner story

One day, Hubert Booth was watching a railway carriage being cleaned with a blowing machine. He noticed that the dust was blown up, but it fell down again so the carriage was not really clean. He came up with the idea of a sucking machine with a filter that trapped the dust. His first vacuum cleaner was a large, horse-drawn, gas-driven machine which was parked outside the building to be cleaned with long hoses being fed through the windows.

The first vacuum cleaners were much bigger than the ones we use today.

Vacuum cleaner timeline

1869	1901	1908	1993
A hand-pumped cleaner was invented by Ives McCaffey in the U.S.	Hubert Booth patents an electric vacuum cleaner in England	James Spangler patents an upright portable vacuum cleaner in the U.S.	James Dyson launches the bagless "cyclone" vacuum cleaner

How vacuum cleaners work

The electric motor in the vacuum cleaner runs a fan. The fan blows air out of the exhaust opening and this creates a partial vacuum inside the cleaner. Air is sucked in, bringing dust and dirt with it. The dust-filled air goes into the vacuum cleaner bag, which traps the dust but lets the air escape out of the exhaust opening.

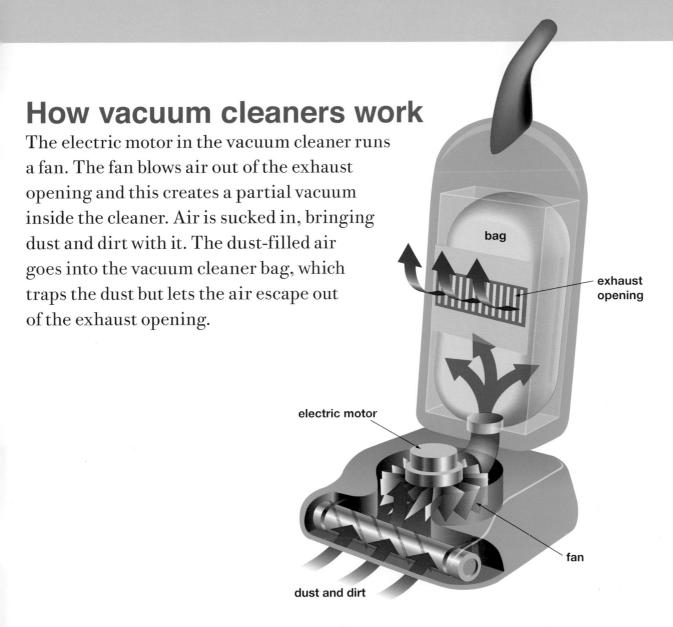

bag

exhaust opening

electric motor

fan

dust and dirt

Changes to vacuum cleaners over time

James Dyson was frustrated whenever his vacuum cleaner became clogged and lost its suction. He spent 15 years experimenting before successfully inventing a "cyclone" vacuum cleaner. It does not have a bag. Instead, the stream of air is sucked in and then made to spin like a cyclone. The dust particles are spun to the walls of the cleaner where they fall to the bottom. This type of cleaner never loses suction.

Related invention
The cordless, hand-held vacuum cleaner was invented in 1979.

Velcro® is a hook and loop fastening system. It has many uses, including on clothing, sports shoes, and wallets.

Who invented Velcro®?

Velcro® was invented by a Swiss man, Georges de Mestral, in 1951.

The Velcro® story

One day in the summer of 1948, Georges de Mestral was walking with his dog in the countryside. Both he and his dog came home covered in burrs, the prickly seed pods from plants they had brushed against. He examined them under a microscope. He saw that the burrs were covered in tiny hooks that latched around the loops of fabric on his trousers. He decided to invent a fastener that worked the same way.

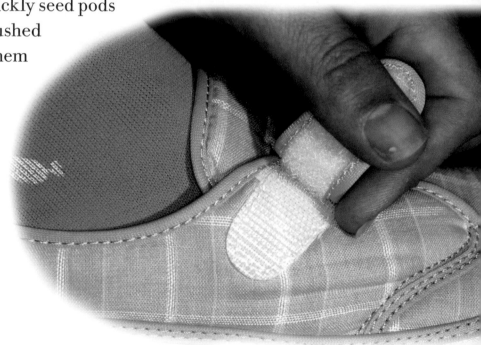

Velcro® can be used on all sorts of clothing.

Georges de Mestral (1907–1990)

Georges de Mestral was born in 1907. As a boy he was interested in nature and inventing. He decided to become an engineer and worked for a Swiss engineering company. After he invented Velcro®, he set up his own company in 1952.

How Velcro® works

One side of the Velcro® is made from tape that has been sewn with nylon. When it is put under a special infrared light, the nylon forms tough hooks. The other side of the tape is sewn with a soft fuzzy material. When the two sides are pressed together, the hooks latch onto the fuzzy loops.

This picture of Velcro® was taken using a microscope.

Changes to Velcro® over time

The first Velcro® tape could only be sewn onto other fabrics. Now it can be stuck onto solid things like notice boards. Space suits have Velcro® fastenings and attachments for tools. The big gloves that astronauts wear make using zippers and buckles impossible, so Velcro® is the perfect solution.

Related invention
Gideon Sundback invented the modern zipper in 1913.

The World Wide Web is a collection of information pages that you can see on your computer by using the Internet.

Who invented the World Wide Web?

The World Wide Web was developed in 1989 by Tim Berners-Lee, an English computer scientist.

The World Wide Web story

In the 1980s, Tim Berners-Lee was working at a physics laboratory in Switzerland. Many different types of computers using different programs were used in the laboratory. You had to log on to each computer to get information. Often it was easier just to go and ask people instead. So Tim Berners-Lee wrote computer programs to take information from one computer system and put it into another. Then he had another idea, to convert every information system to a language that every computer could read, called HTML. That idea led to the creation of the World Wide Web.

Tim Berners-Lee invented the World Wide Web.

Did you know?

In 2003, Tim Berners-Lee was awarded a knighthood by Queen Elizabeth II of England. He can now be called Sir Timothy Berners-Lee.

How the World Wide Web works

Websites are the information pages that you find on the World Wide Web. Each page has its own unique "address" so that you can find it. For example, Tim Berners-Lee's website is at www.w3.org/People/Berners-Lee. (The www in the address stands for World Wide Web.)

All websites are written in the same computer language called hypertext mark-up language (HTML), so everyone can read them. A computer program called a browser searches through millions of pages on the World Wide Web and displays the one you are looking for on your computer.

Web pages are viewed using a browser.

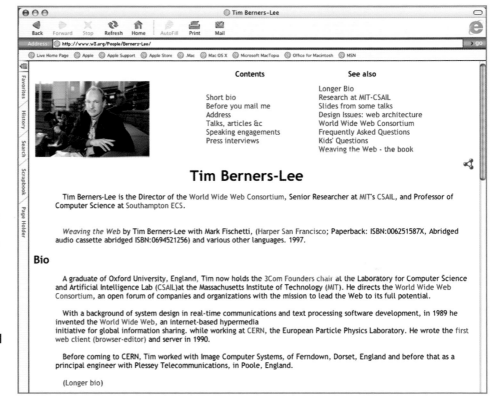

Changes to the World Wide Web over time

In 1993 there were about 620 websites in the world. Today there are more websites than there are people in the world.

Related invention

The Internet is an international network of computers that delivers "packets" of information from one Internet address to another. The Internet was designed by an American computer scientist, Vinton Cerf, in 1973.

X ray

X rays are a type of radiation that can pass through materials that light cannot pass through. They let doctors see inside the human body.

Who discovered X rays?

German scientist, Konrad Roentgen, accidentally discovered X rays in 1895.

The X ray story

Konrad Roentgen noticed some crystals in his laboratory glowed brightly whenever an instrument called a cathode-ray tube was turned on. He decided that the cathode-ray tube must be giving off invisible rays, which he named X rays. "X" meant "unknown."

He studied the rays and noticed that they went easily through some materials such as wood and flesh, but did not travel easily through bone. Within one week of his discovery, Roentgen had taken X ray photographs of his wife's hand. It clearly showed her bones and her wedding ring.

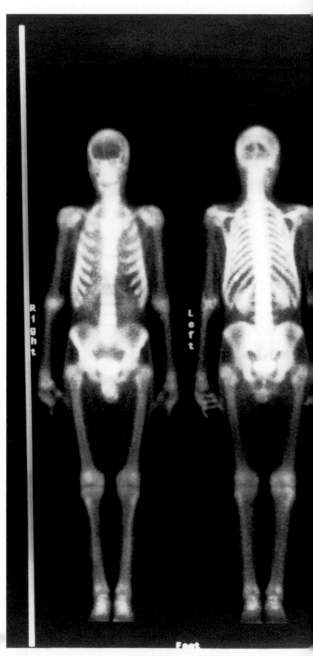

X rays are used in medicine to see inside the body.

Did you know?

In 1964, English archaeologist P. H. K. Gray used X rays to examine 75 Egyptian mummies in the British Museum. Doing this meant he did not have to unwrap them. He discovered that they suffered from arthritis, bad backs, and tooth disease.

How X rays work

X rays are like a high-energy form of light. They are created when fast moving particles called electrons stop as they hit a target in a cathode-ray tube. The picture tube of a television set is a cathode-ray tube. It gives off X rays, which is why you shouldn't sit close to it.

The discovery of X rays was one of the most important moments in modern science. X rays made a big difference to medicine. They were originally used to detect broken bones and foreign objects like swallowed coins.

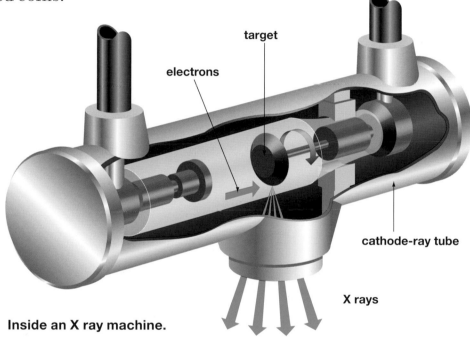

target

electrons

cathode-ray tube

X rays

Inside an X ray machine.

Changes to X rays over time

X rays are used in industry to discover cracks and imperfections in materials. Dentists use X rays to examine the cavities, fillings, and roots of your teeth. Doctors use them to kill some types of cancer cells.

Related invention

Ultrasound imaging was invented by Professor Ian Donald in the 1950s. It uses soundwaves beyond the range of human hearing to make images of tissues inside the human body.

A yo-yo is a toy that has two discs joined in the middle by an axle with a string attached to it.

Who invented the yo-yo?

Pedro Flores is credited with bringing the yo-yo to the U.S. in 1928.

The yo-yo story

Historians believe the yo-yo originated in China about 3,000 years ago. A picture of a boy playing with a yo-yo was also found on an urn that was made in Greece around 500 BCE.

The yo-yo later developed in the Philippines where it was used as a toy and as a weapon. In 1928 a Filipino called Pedro Flores brought the yo-yo to the U.S. He was a hotel bellboy who entertained people with yo-yo tricks. He gave the yo-yo its name (it means "come-come" in Filipino) and set up the Flores Yo-Yo Company.

You can learn to do tricks with a yo-yo.

Did you know?

In 1985, the yo-yo was one of the first toys taken into space by NASA on the Space Shuttle *Discovery*.

How yo-yos work

The simplest kind of yo-yo has two discs joined by an axle. String is wrapped around the axle. When the discs fall, they spin. They keep spinning when they reach the bottom and this winds the string onto the axle again, lifting up the yo-yo. Pulling up on the string gives the yo-yo the extra energy it needs to return to the hand. Different hand actions can make the yo-yo react in a number of ways.

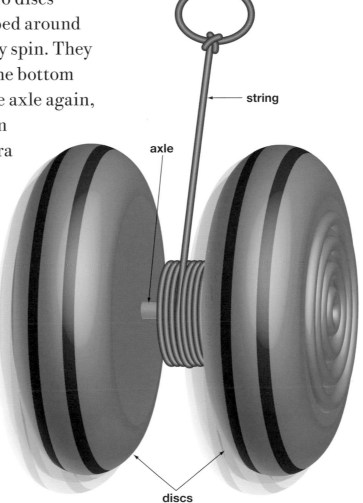

string

axle

discs

Changes to yo-yos over time

The yo-yo is still a very popular toy. Yo-yo competitions are held all over the world. Competitors perform routines to music in front of a panel of judges.

Related invention

French scientist, Leon Foucault, invented the gyroscope in 1852.
A gyroscope has a spinning disc on an axle that is mounted in a frame.

Zippers are devices used to hold together two pieces of material. They have two rows of teeth that can be joined or separated using a sliding clip.

Who invented the zipper?

Whitcomb Judson designed the first interlocking fastener in the early 1890s in the U.S. Gideon Sundback invented the modern zipper in 1913.

The zipper story

Whitcomb Judson's invention had chains of loops and hooks that were joined together by a sliding clasp. He called it the "clasp locker," but it was not very popular.

In 1913 Gideon Sundback, a Swede working in the U.S., adapted Judson's idea to make a smaller and lighter version called the "hookless fastener." The invention really took off when the U.S. Navy used it on its flying suits in 1917.

The invention was called the zipper because of the sound it made.

Zippers keep clothes fastened together.

Zipper timeline

1893	**1913**	**1923**
Whitcomb Judson patented an interlocking fastener called the "clasp locker"	Gideon Sundback patented the modern zipper design	The zipper was first used on rubber boots

How zippers work

A modern zipper has a series of teeth that are clamped onto a strong piece of textile tape. These teeth interlock with another series of teeth on another piece of tape. A sliding clip brings the teeth together or separates them.

Each zipper tooth has a bump on one surface and a hollow on the opposite surface. The bumps and hollows of teeth on opposite tapes fit into each other when the sliding clip brings them together. The teeth cannot come apart because the bumps are too big to fit through the gaps.

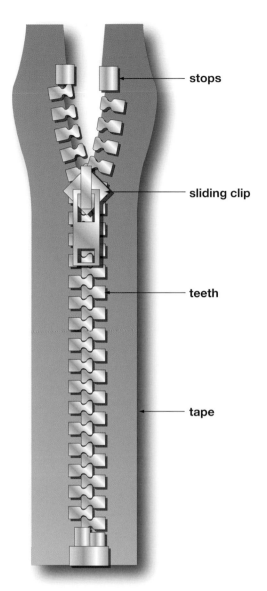

stops

sliding clip

teeth

tape

The sliding clip joins or separates the teeth of a zipper.

Changes to zippers over time

YKK is the world's largest zipper maker. It produces over 1,864 miles (3,000 km) of zippers each day. They are now made in different materials and colors. Doctors can even use a type of zipper to close wounds.

Related invention
Shoelaces and lace holes were invented in England in 1790. Before shoelaces, shoes were usually fastened with buckles.

Index

Page references in bold indicate that there is a full entry for that invention.